THE NEW BEST OF

GEORGE AND IRA GERSHWIN

M000095790

CONTENTS

EMBRACEABLE YOU

Music and Lyrics by
GEORGE GERSHWIN and IRA GERSHWIN

SOMEONE TO WATCH OVER ME

Music and Lyrics by
GEORGE GERSHWIN and IRA GERSHWIN

FASCINATING RHYTHM

Music and Lyrics by
GEORGE GERSHWIN and IRA GERSHWIN

"Fas-ci-nat-ing Rhy-thm You've got me on the go! Fas-ci - nat-ing Rhy-thm I'm all a -

qui - ver. What a mess you're mak-ing! The neigh-bors want to know why I'm

THE MAN I LOVE

Music and Lyrics by
GEORGE GERSHWIN and IRA GERSHWIN

Some-day he'll come a-long   The man I love;   And he'll be big and strong.

The man I love;   And when he comes my way,   I'll do my best to

BUT NOT FOR ME

Music and Lyrics by
GEORGE GERSHWIN and IRA GERSHWIN

SOMEBODY LOVES ME

Words by
BALLARD MacDONALD and B.G. DeSYLVA

Music by
GEORGE GERSHWIN

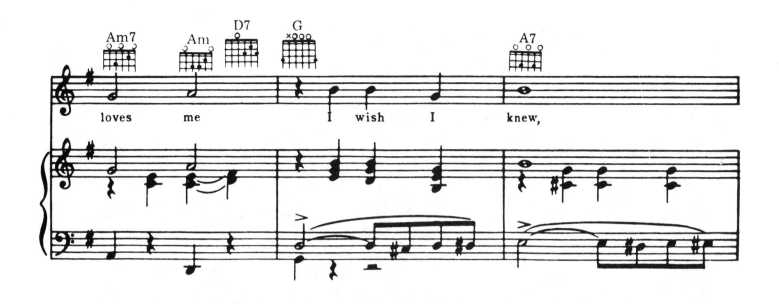

loves me I wish I knew,

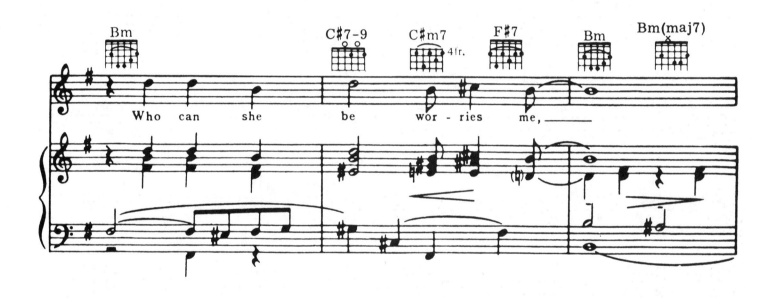

Who can she be wor - ries me,_____

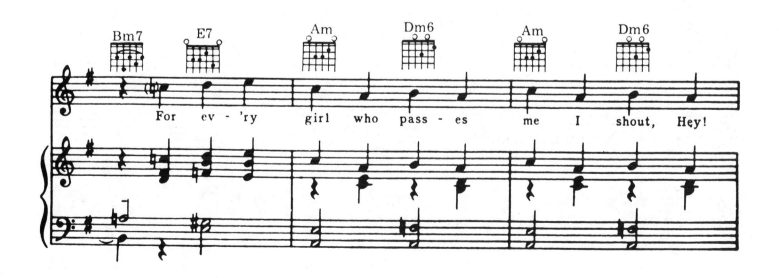

For ev - 'ry girl who pass - es me I shout, Hey!

SOON

Music and Lyrics by
GEORGE GERSHWIN and IRA GERSHWIN

18

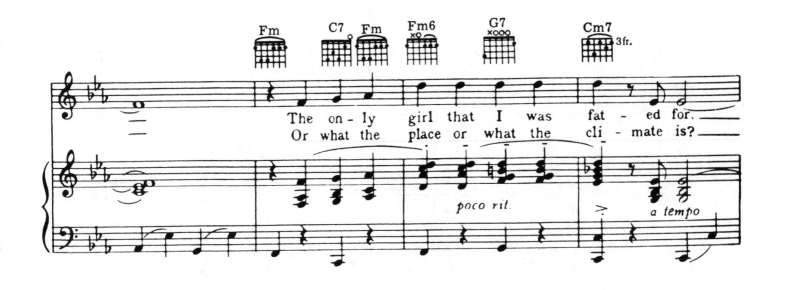

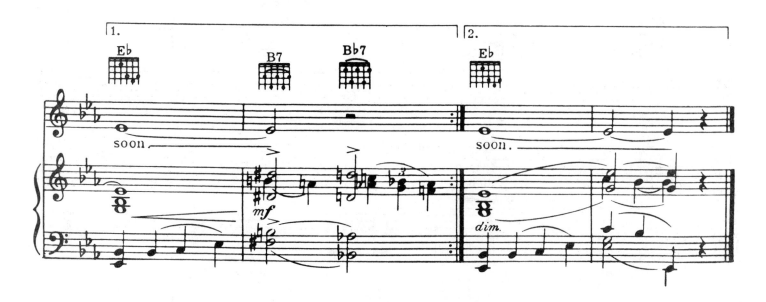

I'VE GOT A CRUSH ON YOU

Music and Lyrics by
GEORGE GERSHWIN and IRA GERSHWIN

BIDIN' MY TIME

Music and Lyrics by
GEORGE GERSHWIN and IRA GERSHWIN

23

I GOT RHYTHM

Music and Lyrics by
GEORGE GERSHWIN and IRA GERSHWIN

LIZA
(All The Clouds'll Roll Away)

Words by
GUS KAHN and IRA GERSHWIN

Music by
GEORGE GERSHWIN

HOW LONG HAS THIS BEEN GOING ON?

Music and Lyrics by
GEORGE GERSHWIN and IRA GERSHWIN

CLAP YO' HANDS

Music and Lyrics by
GEORGE GERSHWIN and IRA GERSHWIN

lose time, Come a-long, it's shake yo' shoes time now for you and me!

On the sands of time you are on-ly a peb-ble;

Re-mem-ber, trou-ble must be treat-ed just like a re-bel,

Send him to the deb-ble! Clap-a yo' hand! Slap-a yo' thigh! Hal-le-lu-yah! Hal-le-

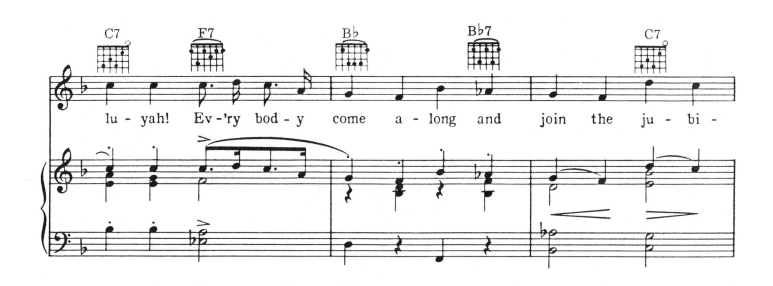

lu - yah! Ev -'ry bod - y come a - long and join the ju - bi -

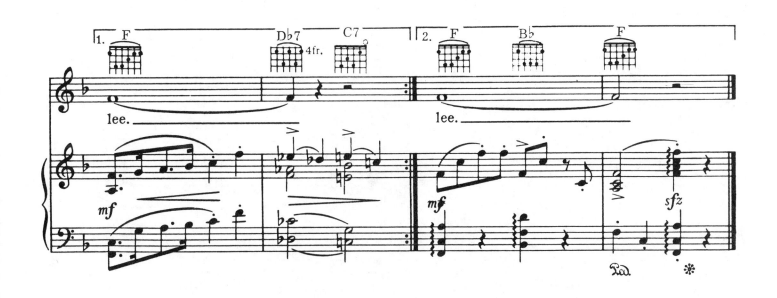

lee. _____ lee. _____

MINE

Music and Lyrics by
GEORGE GERSHWIN and IRA GERSHWIN

36

(1st time counter-melody alone, 2nd time both melodies)

Mine, _____ love is mine, _____

The point they're mak - ing in the song ___ Is that they more than

Wheth - er it's rain or storm or

get a - long, ___ And he is not a - shamed to say ___

shine. _____ Mine, _____ you are mine, ___

She made him what he is to - day. ___ It does a per - son good to see ___

37

DO-DO-DO

Music and Lyrics by
GEORGE GERSHWIN and IRA GERSHWIN

40

OF THEE I SING

Music and Lyrics by
GEORGE GERSHWIN and IRA GERSHWIN

LOVE IS SWEEPING THE COUNTRY

Music and Lyrics by
GEORGE GERSHWIN and IRA GERSHWIN

45

OH, LADY BE GOOD!

Music and Lyrics by
GEORGE GERSHWIN and IRA GERSHWIN

I'LL BUILD A STAIRWAY TO PARADISE

Words by
**B.G. DeSYLVA and
IRA GERSHWIN**

Music by
GEORGE GERSHWIN

SWANEE

Words by
IRVING CAESAR

Music by
GEORGE GERSHWIN

'S WONDERFUL

Music and Lyrics by
GEORGE GERSHWIN and IRA GERSHWIN

STRIKE UP THE BAND!

Music and Lyrics by
GEORGE GERSHWIN and IRA GERSHWIN

© 1927, 1940 WB MUSIC CORP.
Copyrights Renewed
All Rights Reserved

THAT CERTAIN FEELING

Music and Lyrics by
GEORGE GERSHWIN and IRA GERSHWIN

FIDGETY FEET

Music and Lyrics by
GEORGE GERSHWIN and IRA GERSHWIN

LOOKING FOR A BOY

Music and Lyrics by
GEORGE GERSHWIN and IRA GERSHWIN

WHO CARES?
(So Long As You Care For Me)

Music and Lyrics by
GEORGE GERSHWIN and **IRA GERSHWIN**